Marco Hierling, Yu-Chen Yeh, Chloe S.Y. Tai, Jennie Lang Yu

Organizational culture and the case of Google

What is organizational culture and how it can influence the performance of a company

GRIN Verlag

Bibliografische Information der Deutschen Nationalbibliothek:

Die Deutsche Bibliothek verzeichnet diese Publikation in der Deutschen National-
bibliografie; detaillierte bibliografische Daten sind im Internet über http://dnb.d-
nb.de/ abrufbar.

Imprint:

Copyright © 2007 GRIN Verlag GmbH
Druck und Bindung: Books on Demand GmbH, Norderstedt Germany
ISBN: 978-3-640-12690-3

This book at GRIN:

http://www.grin.com/en/e-book/76814/organizational-culture-and-the-case-of-
google

Faculty of Economics and Business

The University of Sydney

Organizational culture and the case of Google

Group Assignment

Organizational Analysis and Behaviour

Handed in by:
Marco Hierling, Yu-Chen Yeh, Chloe S.Y. Tai and Lang Jennie Yu

25th of May 2007

Table of Contents

1. Introduction 3

2. Organizational Culture 4

   2.1 What is organizational culture and what are its key components? 4

   2.2 How is an organisational culture formed? 5

   2.3 Can organisational culture be managed? How does it influence a
firm's performance? 6

3. Google's Organizational Culture 9

   3.1 Short overview – Google Inc. 9

   3.2 The key components and values of Google's culture 9

      3.2.1 Physical Objects 10

      3.2.2 Behaviour Patterns 10

   3.3 Values that lead to creativity and a willingness to perform 12

   3.4 How Google's culture contributes to its success 13

4. Conclusion 15

5. Bibliography 16

1. Introduction

The culture concept evolved to conceptualize humankind's diversity, it asserts that we socially construct different understandings of nature and hence of the reality that surrounds us (Buchanan & Huczynski, 2004). Culture is ubiquitous, exists everywhere and has a significant influence.[1] It affects not only the visible parts of individuals (behaviour and action) but also the invisible ones (beliefs and values). This complex interaction, which takes place on different levels, between individuals and groups within and with other organisations, can be seen as the primary determinant of behaviour in the workplace. The patterns of interaction between people and the external surroundings represent a complex environment which influences behaviour in organisations.

Therefore, more and more managers are talking about changing their culture, creating a new culture, figuring out the impact of their culture, or preserving their culture. In this paper, the main focus is to define organizational culture and determine its influences on companies' performance. Firstly, there are several related questions that will be discussed: What is organizational culture? What are the key elements of it? How is it formed and can it be managed to contribute to a firm's performance? Secondly, we take a closer look at Google's organizational culture and research, to discover whether there is a link between its culture and its performance. Finally, a conclusion is drawn about the culture-performance link and the difficulties associated with this topic.

---

[1] It does not matter where you take a closer look; culture exists everywhere (in families, clubs, schools, companies, cities or even nations) and has a significant influence.

2. Organizational Culture

2.1 What is organizational culture and what are its key components?

There are many definitions of organizational culture, defined by numerous authors. Some see it as 'The way we do things around here' (Deal & Kennedy 1982) while others refer to it as 'something to do with the people and unique quality and style of organization' (Kilmann et al. 1985).[2]

In this paper, Owens' (1987) and Schein's (1990) theories are used to define organizational culture as patterns of shared values and beliefs over time, which produce behavioral norms that are adopted in solving problems. Schein (1985) has also noted that culture is a body of solutions to problems which have worked consistently and are therefore taught to new members as the correct way to perceive, think about, and feel in relation to those problems. In fact, these shared philosophies, assumptions, values, expectations, attitudes, and norms bind an organization together (Kilman et al. 1985). Thus, the set of integrated concepts becomes the manner or strategy through which an organization achieves its specific goals. It can therefore be postulated that an organization's collective culture influences both the attitudes and subsequent behaviors of its employees, as well as the level of performance the organization achieves. The link between performance and culture is seen as critical in the literature, which is addressed later in more detail.

Schein (1990) has noted that culture is thought to permeate the organization on at least three fundamental levels. At the surface, one may observe visible artefacts of the organization, which is, its structure, technology, rules of conduct, dress codes, records, physical layout, stories, and rituals. Beneath this dimension is a second level, organizational values, and, finally, underlying assumptions about the nature of organizational "reality" that are deeper manifestations of values. Of course, investigating processes of culture at the

---

[2] Further, the treatment of culture at the level of the firm varies considerably and its antecedents go back through anthropology, sociology, psychology and early management thought (Needle, 2000, p.101). In general, it is recognized that organisations have 'something' (a personality, philosophy, ideology or climate) which goes beyond economic rationality, and which gives each of them a unique identity.

4

latter level is more difficult, as they cannot be directly observed and measured. With this definition and Schein's three step approach we examine Google's underlying organizational culture and prove if it leads to its performance.

2.2 How is an organisational culture formed?

In general, culture is originated when an organization is started by its founders. They bring the common values and visions into a company which influences how they manage business and the way they recruit new employees. Although corporate founders play an important role in creating and shaping organizational culture (Schein 1992; DeNisi & Griffin 2005).

Buchanan and Huczynski (2004, p.652) point out, that the ultimate strength of a company's culture depends on the homogeneity of group members, as well as, the length and intensity of their shared experiences in a group. At a later stage the process of *organizational socialisation*[3] for new employees plays an important role. New recruits have to be taught to see the organization's world as their more experienced colleagues' do, if the tradition of the organization is to survive (John von Maanen & Edgar Schein 1979). That is achieved through the careful selection of company members, their instruction in appropriate ways of thinking and behaving and the reinforcement of desired behaviours in senior managers.

Since organizational founders have a key impact on culture, they may manage it to achieve the business objectives. However, there is strong debate on this topic, which is addressed next.

---

[3] Organisational socialisation is defined as: The process through which an individual's pattern of behaviour and their values, attitudes and motives are influenced to conform with those seen as desirable in a particular organization (Buchanan and Huczynski, 2004, p.650)

2.3 Can organisational culture be managed? How does it influence a firm's performance?

The controversial debate about whether a strong corporate culture[4] can affect a firm's performance or not is taking place between two camps: The managerial writers and consultants versus the academic social scientists. The managerial view or *functionalist perspective* [5] holds that every organization possesses a culture, just as it has a strategy, structure, technology and employees. Its supporters state that organizational cultures, especially strong ones, are a primary determinant in creating better organizational performances and sustained competitive advantages (Peters & Waterman 1982; Deal & Kennedy 1982; Sadri & Lees 2001; Thompson & McHugh 2002).[6] Strong culture can also underpin stronger organizational commitment, higher moral, more efficient performance, and generally better productivity (Furnham & Gunter, 1993, p.232). They see organizational culture constituting an objective reality of artefacts, values and meanings that academics can quantify and measure. The culture, being an attribute of the organization, is 'given' to its members when they join, and they do not participate in its formation. Culture is acquired by employees, and is thus a variable and hence represents a lever for change which senior management can use (Smircich 1983).

On the other hand, some indicate that culture, does not have a powerful impact on firm's performance. For instance, corporate success is not necessarily attributed to strong cultures (Schlesinger & Balzer 1985; Luthans 1989; Fiol 1991). The view of the social scientists is known as the *symbolic, social constructionist* or *shared cognitions perspective*.[7] They believe that culture

---

[4] Here might the question arise, how a strong culture is defined. Robbins (1996) state that a strong culture provides shared values that ensure that everyone in the organisation is on the same track. Buchanan and Huczynski (2004) define it therefore as consisting of characteristics like the existence of a clear set of values, norms and beliefs, the sharing of these by the great majority of members, and the guidance of employees' behaviour.
[5] Definition from Buchanan and Huczynski, 2004, p.655
[6] The sustained superior performance of firms like IBM, Hewlett-Packard, Proctor and Gamble, and McDonald's may be, at least partly, a reflection of their cultures (Peters & Waterman, 1982).
[7] Definition from Buchanan and Huczynski, 2004, p.655

cannot be easily quantified or measured and state that it is produced and reproduced continuously through the routine interactions between organizational members. Organizational culture is seen as a term that is overused, over-inclusive but under-defined and both its value and its existence as a phenomenon are questioned.

However, this view does not totally reject the influence of leaders, since they are themselves evolved in interactions and thus contribute to culture-shaping. They see it as a way of understanding social relationships within the organisations, and reject the notion that culture may be managed or manipulated (Harris & Ogbonna 1999; Ogbonna 1993).

In this paper we assume that organizational culture has an influence on a firm's performance, but we believe that "strong" culture models, however, oversimplify this relationship. To fulfil the need to accurately analyze culture-performance links, research must combine more appropriate measures of culture's impact with careful attention to intrinsically cultural performance-related organizational processes (Saffold 1988).[8]

Hence, we can conclude that organizational culture can be managed and implemented through managers and contribute to the performance of an organization. But companies are also a source of social relationships and meanings, which are created and recreated in and around the managerial framework (e.g. Vision and Mission)[9], throughout its employees, their routines, and social interactions. "Managers are able to set the direction in which the organization goes, but its employees choose the way they are going".

---

[8] In trait studies, typically, a Sample of excellent or highly productive organizations is selected, and then an attempt is made to identify a "short list" of common cultural characteristics held to explain the superior performance of the sample organizations (Saffold 1988). Further, Pettigrew commented that treated as a static, unitary concept culture "lacks analytical bite." He proposed that it is better to regard culture as "the source of a family of concepts and to explore the roles that symbolism, language, belief, and myth play in creating practical effects" (1985, p. 44).
For example, are there circumstances, as Clark (1980) hypothesized, under which weak cultures are more effective? How would such a finding affect our understanding of strong culture? Perhaps, even more fascinating is the question of how culture functions to suggest parameters for effectiveness.
[9] An example is the role that organisational culture plays in the mission and goal statements. Organisational culture fills the gaps between what is formally announced and what actually takes place. It is the direction indicator that keeps strategy on track (Martins, 2003).

The culture, being an attribute of the organization, is 'given' to its members when they join, but they <u>do</u> participate in its formation and have the ability to influence and change it.

Also Schein's thinking is affiliative in that he acknowledges the existence of a managerial culture, various occupation-based cultures within functional units and worker cultures based on shared hierarchical experiences (Buchanan & Huczynski, 2004, p.657).

3. Google's Organizational Culture

3.1 Short overview – Google Inc.

Google was co-founded by Larry Page and Sergey Brin as a privately held company in 1998, while they were students at Stanford University. The company is specializes in Internet searching and online advertising. It employs about 10,500 full-timers and its mission statement is "to organize the world's information and make it universally accessible and useful" (Google, 2007)[10].

3.2 The key components and values of Google's culture

Google's mission and corporate philosophy, which includes the statements: "You can make money without being evil,"[11] and, "Work should be challenging and the challenge should be fun," illustrates a somewhat more relaxed corporate culture. Hence, it leads to Google's organizational objectives: creating higher productivity, performance, creativity and innovativeness of its products and services (Lee 2006, pp.59-72).

Google believes that an organizational culture and values represent its main spirit, beliefs, assumptions, attitudes and performance; that is, the norms of conduct and values are created by the entire staff in the production processes. This implies that the integrity of employees' values and attitudes towards positive behaviors are very important to Google; such as high loyalty and commitment. Therefore, Google attempts to establish an innovative organizational culture to create a motive power to meet its organizational objectives (Lee 2006, pp.59-72).

Google is famous for its unconventional, risk-taking and relaxed office culture which is operated mainly by its top management. Google's main core value is

---

[10] 10-K Report Google, 2006 and Google (2007), *Corporate Information: Company Overview*, [Online], Available at: http://www.google.com/corporate/ [1st May 2007]
[11] Google's motto: "Don't Be Evil" (Lohr, 2005, C8).

emphasizing 'a belief in people', aligned with its belief that 'people come first' (Lohr 2005, C8). Google's mottos are indicative of its belief in keeping its employees satisfied and enjoying their work leading to greater productivity, as well as, commitment and loyalty toward the company. Thus, the benefits package and working environment must be tailored to its employees to make them 'achieve a good work-life balance which is at the heart of Google's culture' and its slogan: 'happy at work' (Employer Profile–Google, 2005).

Google utilizes its main core value as an 'umbrella' to bring out its other cultural values like: creativity and innovativeness, sincerity and trustworthiness, recognition and performance and a hiring cultural-fit. How Google's unique culture is formed lies amid these core values.

To classify Google's culture, Edgar Schein's three level model (1985, pp.14) of organizational culture in terms of three levels is used. Therefore Google's surface manifestations are structured into two main dimensions which are **physical objects** and **behavior patterns**. These two dimensions are linked to the abovementioned values and beliefs of Google's organizational culture.

3.2.1 Physical Objects

Superior working environment and amenities

Google's management believes that the working environment and a company's culture are the key to attract talents and satisfy employees. Therefore, Google's surface manifestations of its culture include children's day care, financial advice, healthcare, doctors, dry cleaning, massages, haircuts, free food and drink catering, gyms, basketball courts, and also rites like the TGI party and the annual ski trip (Lohr 2005; Lashinky 2007).

3.2.2 Behaviour Patterns

Respect and Equality

Google fosters a low authority and low hierarchy structure which assists the thinking that everyone is equal and should be respected in the company; no one has privileges, even the CEO (Lee 2006, pp.60). The organizational climate is very open and Google provides empowerment and room for employees to do great things (Lohr, 2005, C8). According to Lee (2006), most of the decisions are made collectively through an 'Idea Bank', without much top management interference. [12] Moreover, through a superior project management system everything is kept transparent This assists the objective 360-degree appraisal rather than relying solely on managers' performance assessments (Lee 2006, pp. 62).

20% Time

Google fosters the famous 20% personal time as a norm; this risk-taking culture allows employees to freely spend 'one-day-a-week' on their own selected research projects. This makes the work itself becoming a key attraction and retention tool and establishes creativity and innovativeness in every function (Sullivan 2005; Warner 2004).

Commitments to employees

Basically, Google encourages the values 'sincerity and trustworthiness; this, in turn, encourages employees' to deliver consistent service in the same vein to customers. Further, Google promises that their commitments to their employees benefits, welfare and will never change (Schmidt & Varian 2005; Lee 2006).[13]

Teamwork

Teamwork is a norm in Google's culture and everyone should work together cohesively (Lashinky, 2007, pp.70).

Youth-oriented

Google inclines to provide some unusual perks targeted at its young staff base (Cool Benefits: A Chilled Culture, 2005) [14] . Google's youth-oriented

---

[12] In this 'Idea Bank' everyone can posts his/her ideas which are then voted by all employees themselves to reach agreement.
[13] These management efforts may explain why Google's turnover rate is very low: less than 1% (Lee 2006, pp. 70) and 84% of customers regard Google trustworthy (Godsell, 2007, pp. 1).
[14] Google's quirky touches can be seen from the moment you enter its offices from the fridge in reception containing free soft drinks for staff, to the lava lamps on desks and beanbags and large bouncy balls

organizational culture takes advantage of young employees' willingness to adapt to Google's values and culture.

After analyzing the above mentioned main manifestations of Google's culture, we now explore the intention of Google's management to create and maintain its culture and try to identify the main underlying values.

3.3 Values that lead to creativity and a willingness to perform

The main intention from Google by providing these unusual benefits (physical objects) is to take away stress and increase job security, so that employees' can concentrate on work. Google believes 'it is easy to be penny-wise and pound-foolish with respect to benefits that can save employees considerable time and improve their health and productivity' ('Owner's Manual' 2004). These factors are able to raise the performance of the overall company. Its 20% time norm highlights the employees' personal interests and preferences, which may contribute to employee commitment and high productivity, with the benefit of getting people to think creatively and independently rather than merely stick to company policies and pre-setting goals by management.[15]

Also the strong belief in teamwork stresses the spirit that inspires employees' aspirations to communicate and interact with each other.[16] These factors keep employees satisfied and help them to generate an environment where they can be creative. Google's efforts in highly valuing talents and attracting young people may explain why it always can outperform its competitors and win the talent

---

available as chair substitutes. Employees can also take advantage of an onsite massage chair whenever they feel the need to unwind.
Little quirks can even be found in the more corporate of locations, for example, all meeting rooms are named after famous rock stars including Robert Plant, John Lennon and David Bowie (Employer Profile – Google, 2005).
[15] It is obvious that Google intends to generate the value of creativity and innovativeness from its 20% time rule. In a talk at Stanford University, Marissa Mayer, Google's vice president of search products and user experience, stated that her analysis showed that half of new product launches originated from 20% time.
[16] Moreover, with the effectiveness of teambuilding intervention, managers' roles have been changed, as they are no longer the dictator of decisions; instead, just an aggregators of viewpoints (Schmidt & Varian 2005, E17).

wars.[17] One of Google's core values, recognition and performance, can be observed easily from the three above-mentioned patterns: team work, youth-orientation and highly valuing talents. Google conducts regular job satisfaction surveys and cares for every Googler's feeling toward the company. It believes "People come first" (Russ Cohn states in Employer Profile-Google, 2005) as an important motto by tailoring benefits to people.

3.4 How Google's culture contributes to its success

As Owens (1987) notes, one co-effect of the socialization of organizational values is organizational climate, or the perceptions held by participants as to the nature of the organization. Employees have a variety of perceptions about how well the work environment of the organization is functioning.[18]

It seems that Google's unconventional, innovative, risk-taking and relaxed culture with its emphasis on employee needs contributes significantly to the firms success. However, just how much Google's culture factors contribute to its success and assist it in achieving business goals and objectives, still remains as an arguable question for both management and social scientists. But there are some facts which can be pointed out, it is suggested that both "Google Groups and Google News products are reported to have started as a result of personal 20% time projects." This shows that innovation and creativeness are expected of everyone in every functional unit, not confined within the product development department. Such a "cultural" strategy has driven the company's phenomenal success in product and service innovation. The culture delivers the surrounding to keep employees satisfied and enjoyed at work and at the same time it enables them to be productive and creative while gaining employees' commitment and loyalty.

---

[17] 'Talented people are attracted to Google because we empower them to change the world...Our main benefit is a workplace with important projects, where employees can contribute and grow' (Owner's Manual, 2004).
[18] This includes the quality of social interactions, recognition of their work-related efforts, the types of communication channels open to them, access to technology and resources, and demands or stress placed upon them by the organization (Owens, 1987).

13

Further, Google gives its employees meaning in a greater level, they feel that they are part of something bigger and because of that they are willing to give 110%.[19]

However, attempts from other companies to implement important cultural traits have met with limited success, and academic studies have been sceptical about the culture-performance link and critical of the traits approach itself.[20]

In relation to Google, many analysts are finding that as Google grows, the company is becoming more "corporate". In 2005, articles in The New York Times and other sources began suggesting that Google had lost its anti-corporate, no evil philosophy. In an effort to maintain the company's unique culture, Google has designated a Chief Culture Officer in 2006. His purpose is to develop and maintain the culture and work on ways to keep true to the core values that the company was founded on in the beginning - a flat org

Ultimately, Google has not only succeeded at the stock market; also as employer it is currently very attractive. Its organisational culture and benefits in its work environment are highly valued by employees. The market research study from Universe voted Google, for the first time, as the most preferred employer, displacing McKinsey, which had held this position for the last 12 Years (Rediff News, 2007). It is a magnificent reference to work for Google and therefore employees are willing to work hard. Finally, it looks like Google has found the right way to generate an attractive working environment that is able to motivate their employees and let them have fun at work and in return they honour it with any effort needed.

---

[19] The people at Google, it should be stated, almost universally see themselves as the most interesting people on the planet. Googlers tend to be happy-go-lucky on the outside, but Type A at their core. Ask one what he or she is doing, and it's never "selling ads" or "writing code." No, they are on a quest "to organize the world's information and make it universally accessible and useful." (Lashinky, 2007, p.70).
[20] Thompson and Findlay (1999) cite that management were often not yet able to 'govern the souls' of their employees and staff responses to cultural change initiatives included distancing behaviour, cynicism, deep acting and resigned behavioural compliance rather than internalization of values or attitudes.

4. Conclusion

In fact, researchers have not really identified what specific variables comprise an effective organizational culture, nor have they provided convincing empirical evidence to suggest that if leaders in organizations increased the amount of time and quality of energy devoted to developing a particular type of organizational culture, then an organization would perform at a higher level of productivity (Barney 1986). There is presently little agreement, therefore, about what the concept of organizational culture means or how it should be observed and measured (Schein 1990).[21] Hence, it is unlikely that one will ever obtain a definitive answer.[22]

Overall it is in the interest of both management consultants and managers to maintain that 'culture makes a difference'. Also Google states, that the company thinks a lot about how to maintain their culture and the fun elements. "We spent a lot of time getting our offices right" Mr. Page explains (Vise 2004).[23] And even though it is difficult to measure the influence of strong cultures to organisational success, it is obvious that Google's employees are excited, feel as a part of the company, and are willing to work hard for their most preferred employer.

---

[21] However, attempts from companies to implement traits of strong cultures met with limited success, and academic studies were sceptical about the culture-performance link.
The literature on organizational culture taps essential ideas, but the theory and technology to utilize the theory in improving organizations has remained fuzzy (Mackenzie 1986). As Trice and Beyer (1984) have argued, previous research on organizational culture has tended to focus on single, discrete elements of culture, while ignoring the multidimensional nature of culture, that is, a construct composed of several intimately interrelated variables (Schein 1990). Another problem has been that researchers are still not sure whether the association between culture and organizational performance reflects a "cause-effect" type of relationship (Saffold 1988).
[22] According to Buchanan and Huczynski (2004) that has many reasons: the concept of culture is difficult to operationalise, the factors affecting company performance are many and varied, and isolating the contribution of culture is difficult if not impossible.
[23] Co-founder of Google - Larry Page

5. Bibliography

1. Barney, J. B. (1986), 'Organizational Culture: Can It Be a Source of Sustained Competitive Advantage?', *The Academy of Management Review*, vol. 11, no. 3, July, pp. 656-665.

2. Buchanan, D. and Huczynski, A. (2004), *Organizational Behaviour: An Introductory Text*, 5th edn, Pearson Education Limited, Harlow, Chapter 19, pp. 641-672.

3. Clark, B. (1980) *Academic Culture.* New Haven, CT: Yale Higher Education Research Group.

4. 'Cool benefits: A chilled culture', (2005), *Employee Benefits*, pp.43.

5. Deal, T. E. and Kennedy, A. A. (1982), *Corporate Cultures: The Rites and Rituals of Organization Life*, Addison-Wesley, Reading, MA.

6. DeNisi, A. S. and Griffin, R. W. (2005), *Human Resource Management*, 2nd edition, Houghton Mifflin, Boston.

7. 'EMPLOYER PROFILE - GOOGLE: SEARCHING FOR TALENT', (2005), *Employee Benefits*, October, pp. 66.

8. 'Excerpts From 'Owner's Manual' Included With Offering', (2004), *The New York Times*, pp. C.7.

9. Fiol, C. M. (1991), 'Managing Culture as a Competitive Resource: An Identity-Based View of Sustainable Competitive Advantage', *Journal of Management*, vol. 17, no. 1, March, pp. 191-211.

10. Godsell, M. (2007), 'Why should we trust you?', *Marketing*, pp.16.

11. 'EMPLOYER PROFILE - GOOGLE: SEARCHING FOR TALENT', (2005), *Employee Benefits*, October, pp. 66.

12. Harris, L. C. and Ogbonna, E. (1999), 'Developing a Market Oriented Culture: A Critical Evaluation', *Journal of Management Studies*, vol. 36, no. 2, March, pp. 177-196.

13. John von Maanen and Edgar Schein, (1979) - Out of Buchanan and Huczynski, 2004, *Organizational Behaviour: An Introductory Text*, pp.650.

14. Kilmann, R. H., Saxton, M. J., Serpa, R. and Associates (1985), *Gaining Control of the Corporate Culture*, Jossey-Bass, San Francisco, CA.

15. Lashinky, A. (2006), 'Chaos by Design', *Fortune*, vol.154, no.7, pp. 86.

16. Lashinky, A. (2007), 'Search and enjoy', *Fortune*, vol.155, no.1, pp. 70.

17. Lee, K. F. (2006), *Becoming 21st Century Talent*, Linking, Taiwan.

18. Lohr, S. (2005), 'At Google, Cube Culture Has New Rules', *The New York Times*, pp. C.8.

19. Luthans, F. (1989), 'Conversations with Edgar H. Schein', *Organizational Dynamics*, vol. 17, no. 4, Spring, pp. 60-76.

20. Martins, E. C. and Terblanche, F. (2003), 'Building organisational culture that stimulates creativity and innovation', *European Journal of Innovation Management*, vol. 6, no. 1, pp. 64-74.

21. Needle, D. (2000), 'Culture at the level of the firm: organizational and corporate perspectives', in Jim Barry, John Chandler, Heather Clark, Roger Johnston and David Needle (eds), *Organisation and Management: A critical text*, Thomson Learning Business Press, pp.101

22. Ogbonna, E. (1993), 'Managing Organisational Culture: Fantasy or Reality?', *Human Resource Management Journal*, vol. 3, no. 2, pp. 42-54.

23. Owens, R. (1987), *Organizational Behavior in Education*, Englewood Cliffs, NJ: Prentice-Hall.

24. Peters, T. J. and Waterman, R. H. (1982), *In Search of Excellence: Lessons from America's Best Run Company*, Harper & Row, New York.

25. Pettigrew, A. (1985), *The awakening giant*. Oxford, England: Basil Blackwell.

26. Robbins, S.P. (1996), *Organizational Behaviour: Concepts, Controversies, Applications*, 7th edn, Prentice-Hall, Englewood Cliffs, NJ, .

27. Sadri, G. and Lees, B. (2001), 'Developing Corporate Culture as a Competitive Advantage', *Journal of Management Development*, vol. 20, no. 10, pp. 853-859.

28. Saffold, G. S. (1988), 'Culture Traits, Strength, and Organizational Performance: Moving Beyond "Strong" Culture', *Academy of Management Review*, vol.13, no. 4, pp.546-558.

29. Schein, E. H. (1985), *Organizational Culture and Leadership*, San Francisco: Jossey-Bass. (1990), "Organizational Culture," *American Psychologist*, vol. 45, no.2, pp.109-119.

30. Schein, E. H. (1988), 'Innovative Cultures and Organizations', *Management in the 1990s*, Sloan School of Management, Massachusetts Institute of Technology, November.

31. Schein, E. H. (1992), *Organizational Culture and Leadership*, 2nd edn, Jossey-Bass, San Francisco, Chapter 11, pp. 211-227.

32. Schlesinger, L. A. and Balzer, R. J. (1985), 'An Alternative to Buzzword Management: The Culture-Performance Link', *Personnel*, vol. 62, no. 9, September, pp. 45-51.

33. Schmidt, E. and Varian, H. (2005), 'The Google Workout', *Newsweek*, vol. 146, no.25, E17.

34. Smircich, L. (1983) – 'Concepts of culture and organizational analysis', *Administrative Science Quarterly,* 28, pp. 339-358.

35. Sullivan, J. (2005), *'A Case Study of Google Recruiting-Can any firm compete against this recruiting machine?',* [Online], Available: http://www.ere.net/articles/db/06465389A59D4E0FAA6F0EFFD4A78126.asp [19th May 2007].

36. Thompson, P. and McHugh, D. (2002), *Work Organization: A Critical Introduction,* 3rd edn, Palgrave Basingstoke.

37. Warner, M. (2004), 'Google's wisdom and culture', *Business 2.0,* vol. 5, no.5, pp. 100.

38. Google (2007), *Corporate Information: Company Overview,* [Online], Available: http://www.google.com/corporate/ [1st May 2007]

39. Mills, E. (2007) "Meet Google's culture czar", ZDNet, April 30, 2007, http://www.zdnet.com.au/insight/software/soa/Meet-Google-s-culture-czar/0,139 023769,339275147,00.htm

40. Rediff News (2007) Google: Best workplace for MBA grads, May 04, 2007, http://inhome.rediff.com/money/2007/may/04google.htm

41. Sueddeutsche Newspaper (2007) Google als Arbeitgeber, "Traumfirma für jeden MBA", 06.05.2007, http://www.sueddeutsche.de/wirtschaft/artikel/773/112661/

42. Vise, D. A. "Tactics of 'Google Guys' Test IPO Law's Limits." Washington Post, August 17, 2004, http://www.washingtonpost.com/wp-dyn/articles/A6742-2004Aug16.html